Jan 2 -

A FEW ROYAL OCCASIONS

Selected by
SUE BRADBURY
and with an introduction by
JOHN LETTS

Advice to a courtier: *Speak well of everyone, ask for everything that's going and sit down when you get the chance . . .*

LONDON
The Folio Press
MCMLXXVII

PRINTED IN GREAT BRITAIN
by W & J Mackay Limited, Chatham
Set in 11 *point Ehrhardt leaded* 1 *point*

CONTENTS

INTRODUCTION

'Being royal has many painfull drawbacks' wrote Daisy Ashford in *The Young Visiters*. Not the least of the drawbacks, one imagines, must be the literally inexhaustible curiosity most of us retain about matters royal. This must surely stem only marginally from snobbishness. The truth is that royalty has the most desirable and collectable attribute of all – extreme rarity value. Hence the eternal compulsion to record how it was in particular royal circles, and what *they* were like. We invent a myth to suit ourselves, for social and almost mythical reasons, and become so convinced by it that we read endless memoirs written to reassure us that the myth has reality. Like the rich, kings and queens are different from us. But, unlike the rich, it is because we make them so, and not they.

Here we add our mite to the massive sum that has already come and gone in this year of Jubilee, and offer a little anthology, chosen from some sixteen of the four hundred or so books published by The Folio Society in the last thirty years. It covers many royal occasions, and over a thousand years of English kings and queens, from King Vortigern and Hengist and Horsa in the Dark Ages to some leaves from Queen Victoria's own *Highland Journal*. Most of the quotations here come from first-hand sources. They are often the raw material for those memorable sentences in the history books of our schooldays. And, very often, they are much more vivid in their raw state than after mastication and digestion by learned historians. Keeping to the plan of limiting this little collection to quotations from books we have published, many now, unhappily, out of print, we find inevitably that there are enormous gaps. A pageant it turns out to be – but a rather unbalanced pageant. There is much here of Henry VIII and Elizabeth I, who after three and a half centuries, still tower over all the other characters in a glittering caste. The Stuarts are well represented, and also the Georges. There is much ceremony and spectacle: coronations and *levées*, banquets and marriages, processions and audiences. There is feasting of *every* kind, in all styles from the splendid to the merely magnificent. There is also a great deal of hilarity, much farce, some shrewd observation and a certain amount of low comedy. Added to that, there is, here and there, some pathos, and a few deaths: some in battle, like King Harold, and some at the scaffold, such as King Charles I. Perhaps the most authentic *frisson* of all comes from George Cavendish. Cavendish was Cardinal Wolsey's steward, and the account he has left us of his cross-examination by Henry VIII after his master's disgrace and death is one that makes the mouth go dry and the heart to beat faster even today, nearly four hundred years after the incident happened. It must surely be the most vivid glimpse of our royal past of all . . . except for – and one must now pay tribute to virtually *all* the writers who left us these incomparable scraps from the rich men's tables.

They are *all* fascinating, still. As Dr Lewis Thorpe says, Geoffrey of Monmouth's *History of the Kings of Britain* is unacceptable as history, in the main – 'and yet history keeps peeping through the fiction'. Much the same is true of William of Poitiers, who left us the earliest account of the Norman invasion and the Battle of Hastings. Surely the paragraphs quoted here are as real as any report from any battlefield. Whatever the truth of these early records, with Hall's *Chronicles* we are on firmer ground. The glittering account he has given us of the arrival of Anne of Cleves – 'the Flanders mare' – in England for her marriage to Henry is reporting of a high order for any age, and would not have disgraced any skilled journalist of today.

Next come a group of more personal memoirs, first among them Sir James Melville of Halhill, whose declared intention was to set down only 'such things as I myself was employed in, or where I was present and heard with my ears'! Melville made himself present, amongst other places, in Queen Elizabeth's bedchamber and her audience room – at some risk, one imagines; and his record of what he saw and heard shows him to be as skilful a diplomat as he was an accurate observer. Next is the cheerful and irreverent Sir John Harington, courtier, dilettante, inventor, so it is said, of the water closet. He was godson to Queen Elizabeth herself – 'Go tell that witty fellow, my godson, to get home: it is no season now to fool it here' she once is reported to have said. His account of the hilarious masque given by King James I for his alcoholic brother-in-law Christian IV of Denmark, is a classic piece of elegant irreverence.

From here we come to the great ages of memoir and anecdote, and to those endearing masterpieces of John Aubrey, that strange eccentric, and John Evelyn, one of our two great diarists; and, by easy and entertaining stages, to the more overtly decadent regency. Here we meet in Thomas Creevey our master gossip, and, in the dapper Captain Gronow, perhaps England's foremost exponent of the art of the *raconteur*.

Opinions may differ about the place of the first four Georges in the pantheon of our monarchy, but surely no one can deny the supremacy of their reign as our finest source of anecdote, gossip and scandal. Some of the stories remain in occasional use today – for instance Brummell's famous insult to the Prince Regent, when he turned to his host, on seeing the Prince approaching and blandly asked 'Who is your fat friend?' As Gronow records, life punished Brummell roundly for his insolence – 'At last he got himself named consul at Caen, but he afterwards lost the appointment, and eventually died insane and in abject poverty at Calais.'

Of ludicrous occasions, there is perhaps nothing more striking in English history than the scene at Westminster Abbey, on 19 July 1821, when George IV's queen was refused admission to her own coronation by the doorkeeper at The House of Lords. The doorkeeper said, that his instructions were to admit no person without a Peer's ticket. Lord Hood – 'Did you ever hear of a Queen being asked for a ticket before? This is your Queen.' The doorkeeper (perhaps an earlier incarnation of today's traffic warden) said that 'his orders were general, and without any exceptions'. (He added that he had never been in a similar situation before, and could therefore say nothing as to the propriety or impropriety of refusing her Majesty admission).

This graphic scene comes from Nightingale's *Memoirs of The Public and Private Life of Queen Caroline* – known on commemorative mugs and plates, not unreasonably, as The Injured Queen of England.

Creevey, too, was a natural, untaught painter in words. In a few sentences, he had the gift of conveying precise impressions more deftly than any professional historian. As . . . 'I have been much disappointed today with the *levée* . . . There was nothing interesting or imposing about it. A vast crowd, with barely standing room, for two hours: afterwards moved to the Presence Chamber, where no one was for a minute . . . The king did not seem to move a muscle, and we all asked each other, when we came away, what had made us take so much trouble.'

The answer to Creevey's comment can come as aptly, perhaps, once more from Daisy Ashford as anywhere. 'What I say is what dose it matter, we can't all be of royal blood, can we?'

JOHN LETTS

KING VORTIGERN and KING ARTHUR

From The History of the Kings of Britain *by Geoffrey of Monmouth.*

The historical facts may be suspect, but the stories of Vortigern and Arthur, culled from the legends of the Dark Ages, contain elements which recur through the reigns of many more reliably recorded monarchs: battles, rewards, punishments, diplomacy, low cunning, feasting, conspiracy, death – the power of women and the pageantry of power.

Once he had won this victory with the help of the Saxons, Vortigern increased his gifts to them. To their leader Hengist he gave many lands in the neighbourhood of Lindsey, so that he could maintain himself and his fellow-soldiers. Hengist was a clever man and an astute one. When he came to understand the friendship which the king bore him, he went to him and made the following request to him: 'My lord, on every side your enemies are harassing you yourself and also those of your fellow-countrymen who have any love for you. They are all threatening that they will recall Aurelius Ambrosius from the land of Armorica, so that they can depose you and make him king in your place. If you agree, let us send to our own country and invite more soldiers to come from there, so that our own battle-strength may be increased. There is, too, one other boon that I would ask of you in your clemency, if I did not fear to have it refused to me.' 'Send your messengers to Germany,' answered Vortigern, 'and invite as many men as you have thought necessary. Then ask of me what you will, for it will not be refused to you' . . . 'I am your servant,' replied Hengist. 'Grant me, then, within the territory which you have assigned to me, as much land as can be encircled by a single thong, so that I can build there a fortress into which I may retreat in time of need. I am your faithful liege. I have been so in the past and I shall remain so in the future. What I propose to do I shall carry out in all fidelity to you.' The king was moved by the words of Hengist. He granted him his request and ordered him to send messengers to Germany, so that the soldiers could be summoned from that country and come quickly to bring help. Hengist immediately sent representatives to Germany. He then took the hide of a bull and cut it into a single leather thong. With this thong he marked out a certain precipitous site which he had chosen with the greatest possible cunning. Inside the space which he had measured he began to build a fortress.

Meanwhile the messengers returned from Germany, bringing with them eighteen ships full of carefully picked soldiers.

They also brought with them the daughter of Hengist, a girl called Renwein, whose beauty seemed second to none. Once they had arrived, Hengist invited King Vortigern to his home to inspect the new building and to review the warriors who had just landed. The king came there incognito. He praised the fortress which had been built so quickly and he took into his service the soldiers whom Hengist had summoned. While he was being entertained at a royal banquet, the girl Renwein came out of an inner room carrying a golden goblet full of wine. She walked up to the king, curtsied low and said: '*Laverd King, was hail!*' When he saw the girl's face, Vortigern was greatly struck by her beauty and was filled with desire for her. He asked his interpreter what it was that the girl had said and what he ought to reply to her. 'She called you Lord King,' answered the interpreter, 'and did you honour by drinking your health. What you should reply is "*drinc hail*".' Vortigern immediately said the words '*drinc hail*' and ordered Renwein to drink. Then he took the goblet from her hand, kissed her and drank in his turn. From that day to this the tradition has endured in Britain that the one who drinks first at a banquet says '*was hail*' to his partner and he who takes the drink next replies '*drinc hail*'.

Vortigern was tipsy from the mixture of drinks which he had consumed. Satan entered his heart, so that he fell in love with Renwein and asked her father to give her to him. I say that Satan entered his heart because, despite the fact that he was a Christian, he was determined to make love with this pagan woman. Hengist, who was a very clever man, immediately noticed the unbalanced nature of the king's personality. He consulted his brother Horsa and the other senior men who were around him as to what he should do about the king's request. They agreed unanimously that the girl should be handed over to the king and that in exchange for her they should demand the province of Kent.

No time was wasted. Renwein was given to Vortigern and the province of Kent to Hengist: this last without the knowledge of Earl Gorangonus who ruled over the territory. The king was married to the pagan woman that very night and she pleased him beyond all measure.

'... *And thus it passed ... that the month of May was come, when every lusty heart beginneth to blossom ...*'

Malory: *Morte d'Arthur*

When the feast of Whitsuntide began to draw near, Arthur, who was quite overjoyed by his great success, made up his mind to hold a plenary court at that season and place the crown of the kingdom on his head. He decided, too, to summon to this feast the leaders who owed him homage, so that he could celebrate Whitsun with greater reverence and renew the closest possible pacts of peace with his chieftains. He explained to the members of his court what he was proposing to do and accepted their advice that he should carry out his plan in the City of the Legions ...

Messengers were sent to the different kingdoms and invitations were delivered to all those who were due to come to the court from the various parts of Gaul and from the near-by Islands in the Sea ...

All marched with a train of accoutrements, mules and horses such as I find it hard to describe. Once they are listed, there remained no prince of any distinction this side of Spain who did not come when he received his invitation. There was nothing remarkable in this: for Arthur's generosity was known throughout the whole world and this made all men love him.

Finally, when they had all assembled in the town and the time of the feast had come, the archbishops were led forward to the palace, so that they could place the royal crown upon the king's head. Since the plenary court was being held in his own diocese, Dubricius made ready to sing mass in celebration of the moment when the king should place the crown upon his head. As soon as the king was enrobed, he was conducted with due pomp to the church of the metropolitan see. On his right side and on his left there were two archbishops to support him. Four kings, of Albany, Cornwall, Demetia and Venedotia, preceded him, as was their right, bearing before him four golden swords. A company of clerics of every rank advanced before him, chanting in exquisite harmony.

From another direction the archbishops and bishops led the queen, adorned with her own regalia, to the church of the dedicated virgins. Before her walked the four consorts of the kings already mentioned, carrying four white doves according to the custom. All the married women present followed behind her with great rejoicing.

Afterwards, when the procession was over, so much organ music was played in the two churches and the choirs sang so sweetly that, because of the high standard of the music offered, the knights who were there hardly knew which of the churches to enter first. They flocked in crowds, first to this one, then to the other, so that if the whole day had been spent in celebration they would not have been bored. Finally, high mass was celebrated in both churches.

The king and the queen took off their crowns and put on lighter regalia. The king went off with the men to feast in his own palace and the queen retired with the married women to feast in hers; for the Britons still observed the ancient custom of Troy, the men celebrating festive occasions with their fellow-men and the women eating separately with the other women. When they were all seated as the rank of each decreed, Kay the Seneschal, robed in ermine and assisted by a thousand noblemen who were all clad in ermine too, bore in the food. The same number of men, clad this time in minever, followed Bedevere the Cup-bearer from another entrance, helping him to pass drinks of all sorts in goblets of every conceivable shape. Meanwhile, in the queen's palace, innumerable servants, dressed in varying liveries, were performing their duties, each according to his office.

If I were to describe everything, I should make this story far too long. Indeed, by this time, Britain had reached such a standard of sophistication that it excelled all other kingdoms in its general affluence, the richness of its decorations, and the courteous behaviour of its inhabitants. Every knight in the country who was in any way famed for his bravery wore livery and arms showing his own distinctive colour; and women of fashion often displayed the same colours. They scorned to give their love to any man who had not proved himself three times in battle. In this way the womenfolk became chaste and more virtuous and for their love the knights were ever more daring.

Invigorated by the food and drink which they had consumed, they went out into the meadows outside the city and split up into groups ready to play various games. The knights planned an imitation battle and competed together on horseback, while their womenfolk watched from the top of the city walls and aroused them to passionate excitement by their flirtatious behaviour. The others passed what remained of the day in shooting with bows and arrows, hurling the lance, tossing heavy stones and rocks, playing dice and an immense variety of other games: this without the slightest show of ill-feeling. Whoever won his particular game was then rewarded by Arthur with an immense prize. The next three days were passed in this way. On the fourth day all those who in the office which they held had done Arthur any service were called together and each rewarded with a personal grant of cities, castles, archbishoprics, bishoprics and other landed possessions.

KING HAROLD and WILLIAM THE CONQUEROR (1027–1087)

From The History of William, Duke of the Normans and King of the English c. *1073/4, by William of Poitiers, translated by Lewis Thorpe for* The Bayeux Tapestry.

William of Poitiers wrote by far the most complete account of the happenings depicted in the Bayeux Tapestry, and his summing up after the Battle of Hastings is a moving picture of the passing of the last of the Saxon kings.

Once he had completed his victory, the duke rode back to the battlefield to survey the dead. The flower of English youth and nobility littered the ground far and wide. At the king's side they found his two brothers. Harold was recognized, not by any insignia which he wore and certainly not from his features, but by certain distinguishing marks. They carried his body to Williams' camp and it was handed over for burial to William, surnamed Malet. The duke refused to give the corpse to Harold's mother, although she offered an equal weight of gold for the remains of her son whom she loved so much. He fully realized how unseemly it would have been to have accepted gold in exchange in this way. He was quite convinced that it would have been wrong to have allowed Harold to be buried as his mother wished, for as the result of his boundless ambition innumerable men lay dead and uninterred. They said jokingly that his body should be placed there in position to guard the sea-shore and the ocean, which, in his fury, he had till then invested with his arms.

We Normans offer you no insult, Harold: rather we pity you and weep to see your fate, we and the pious Conqueror, who was saddened by your fall. You won such measure of success as you deserved, and then, again as you deserved, you met your death, bathed in your own heart's blood. Now you lie there, in your grave by the sea: by generations yet unborn of English and of Normans you will ever be accursed. So must fall those who in great earthly power seek their own supreme good, who rejoice only when usurping it, who, once that it is seized, strive to retain it by the force of arms. . . . The cataclysm which you caused dragged you down in its wake. You shine no more beneath the crown which you so wrongfully usurped; you sit no longer on the throne to which you proudly climbed. Your last expiring moments proved if it were right or wrong for you to be exalted by this gift made by King Edward as he died. That comet, terror of all kings, which gleamed so bright when you were newly crowned, was but a presage of your own defeat.

HENRY II
(b. 1133, reigned 1154–1189)

From The Life and Death of Thomas Becket *by William fitzStephen, clerk to Thomas Becket, Chancellor of England and Archbishop of Canterbury.*

By the time Henry II came to the throne a clash between Church and State was imminent. Perhaps Henry hoped to diffuse matters by appointing his best friend to the highest ecclesiastical office, that of Archbishop of Canterbury. Instead, Becket opposed him implacably, prompting the king's famous outburst: 'What a parcel of fools and dastards have I nourished in my house that not one of them will avenge me of this one upstart clerk!' Some of his barons obliged and Thomas was murdered in his own cathedral.

When the daily round of business had been dealt with, the king and Thomas would sport together like boys of the same age, in hall, in church, and while sitting or riding abroad. One day they were riding together through the streets of London. It was a hard winter and the king observed an old man approaching, poor and clad in a thin and ragged coat. 'Do you see that man?' said the king to the chancellor. 'Yes, I see him,' replied the chancellor. 'How poor he is, how feeble, how scantily clad!' said the king. 'Would it not be an act of charity to give him a thick warm cloak?' 'It would indeed, and you, O king, ought to have a mind and an eye to it.' In the meantime the poor man came up to them. The king and the chancellor both stopped. The king greeted him pleasantly and asked him if he would like a good cloak. The poor man, not knowing who they were, thought this was a jest and not meant to be taken seriously. Said the king to the chancellor, 'You shall have the credit of this act of charity', and laying hands on his hood he tried to pull off the cape the chancellor was wearing, a new and very good one of scarlet and grey, which he struggled hard to keep. A great din and commotion then arose, and the knights and nobles in their train hastened up wondering what was the cause of this sudden strife between them. But no one could tell. Both of them had their hands fully occupied, and more than once seemed likely to fall off their horses. At last the chancellor reluctantly allowed the king to overcome him, and suffered him to pull the cape from his shoulders and give it to the poor man. The king then explained what had happened to his attendants. They all laughed loudly, and some of them offered their own capes and cloaks to the chancellor. The poor old man walked off with the chancellor's cape, joyful and rich beyond expectation, and giving thanks to God.

Oft-times the king would come to dine at the chancellor's house, sometimes for the sake of sport, at other times to see whether what was said about his household and table was true. Sometimes the king, bow in hand, as he returned from the hunt or was about to set off, rode on horseback into the hall where the chancellor sat at table; sometimes he would take a drink and depart when he had seen him: sometimes he would jump over the table and sit down to meat with him. Never in the whole Christian era were two men more of one mind or better friends.

Becket flees the Council of Northampton:

The bishops then returned to the king. Being excused by him from judging the archbishop, they took their seats apart from the barons. Nevertheless the king demanded judgment on the archbishops from the earls and barons. Certain sheriffs and barons of the second rank [i.e. *barones minores*], men full of years, were also summoned to join them in the judgment. After some little delay the magnates returned to the archbishop. Robert, Earl of Leicester, who in age and rank excelled the rest, tried to depute the promulgation of sentence to others. When they refused, he began to recapitulate the business enacted at Clarendon point by point, but Hilary, Bishop of Chichester, grimly interrupted him, crying out that the archbishop was clearly guilty of treason through his breach of the promise made there *in word of truth*, and signified to him that he must hear the sentence. But the archbishop could endure no more and said, 'What is this which you would do? Are you come to judge me? You have no right to do so. Judgment is a sentence given after trial, and this day I have said nothing in formal pleading. For no suit have I been summoned hither, save only at the suit of John [the marshal], who has not come to prove his charges. With respect to this you cannot pass sentence. Such as I am, I am your father, and you are magnates of the household, lay powers, secular personages. I will not hear your judgment'.

The magnates then retired. A little later the archbishop arose and, carrying his cross, made for the door, which had all day been securely fastened, but now opened as though of its own accord. A certain man pursued him, slandering him as he went, calling him a perjurer: another cried out that he fled like a traitor and carried the king's sentence with him . . .

Becket returned to England on 24 November 1170.
At length the archbishop arrived at the port of Wissant. The face of the sea and the sky was calm, the archbishop's ship was ready for him and some of the others were already under way. The archbishop stood there waiting. Some of his clerks, his fellow-exiles, all agog to set foot again on their native soil, called out to him, 'Look, my lord, we can see England! The sails of the other ships are swelling in the breeze. Why do you not embark? Shall we be like Moses, who gazed on the land of promise, but did not enter in?' 'Why are you in such a hurry?' he replied: 'within forty days of your landing you will wish you were anywhere else in the world but in England.'

EDWARD IV
(b. 1442, reigned 1461–1470 and 1471–1483)

From the Memoirs *of Philippe de Commynes, translated by Paul Kendall under the title* The Universal Spider.

As counsellor to Louis XI of France, Philippe de Commynes was admirably placed to witness his king's dealings with the English following the invasion of 1475. Ironic, racy and grave by turns, Commynes had a highly developed sense of the ridiculous, apparent in this, an early account of 'the English abroad'.

To put the finishing touches on the truce, the King of England [and his army] moved to the vicinity of Amiens, encamping half a league [downstream on the right bank of the Somme] from that city. Louis XI, who had been able to see them approaching from afar, stationed himself at the city gate. In truth, the English appeared to have little experience in the art of campaigning, and they rode in disorder. The king sent the King of England three hundred wagons loaded with the best wines that could be found; the wagon train seemed to be an army almost as large as that of England. It being a time of truce, many Englishmen came into Amiens. They behaved foolishly and showed little respect for their king. They came fully armed, and in large companies; and had our king wished to act in bad faith, never could such a quantity of men have been destroyed so easily. But the king thought only of making them good cheer and establishing a peace with England that would last his lifetime.

He had ordered two huge tables to be set up outside the town gate, one on each side; they were laden with all kinds of things to eat that provoke thirst and with the best wines obtainable, and there were people to serve. Of water, there was no news. At each of the tables the king had seated five or six men of rank, large and fat men, in order to create an atmosphere of conviviality . . . As the English approached the gate, they beheld this array; people took their horses' reins, saying that they should run a course in the lists there, and brought them to the tables, where they were treated to all that the scene offered; and they were very happy with the programme.

Whatever place they chose to enter, once they had gone within the town, they paid nothing. There were nine or ten taverns well stocked with the needful, where they went to eat and drink; and whatever they asked for was served them without charge. This situation lasted three or four days . . .

On the morning to which I refer, as the king rose and was saying his hours, someone came to tell me that there were at least nine thousand English in the town . . .

The king was not at all obstinate. He immediately left off saying his hours, telling me that it was not necessary to observe the ceremony of the Innocents that day, and ordered me to mount horse and try to speak with some of the English captains to see if we could get the English out of the town. I spoke to three or four English captains whom I knew, explaining the matter as the situation called for. For every Englishman they ordered out of the town, however, twenty entered it. The king sent after me the lord de Gié, now Marshal of France. In order to investigate, we entered a tavern – a hundred and eleven servings had already been chalked up and it was not yet nine o'clock in the morning. The house was full: some were drunkenly singing and some were in drunken slumber . . .

The King of England, informed of this disorder, was ashamed of it. In a message to the king he asked that orders be given for none of his men to be admitted. The king made reply that this he would never do; however, if the King of England wished to, he should send some of his archers to take over the guarding of the gate and admit whomever they pleased. Thus was it done. And a great many English left the town by order of the King of England.

It was then decided that, to bring all matters to an end, a place must be chosen where the two kings would meet and men must be appointed to make the selection. My lord du Bouchage and I represented the king on this mission and my lord Howard, a man named St Leger and a herald acted for the King of England. After we had inspected the banks of the Somme river, we agreed that the best and most secure place for the meeting was Picquigny, three leagues [downstream] from Amiens, a stronghold belonging to the Vidame of Amiens, though it had been burned [in 1471] by the Duke of Burgundy. The town lies low on the river Somme, which is not fordable and, at this spot, is not wide.

On the route the king would take to come there [along the left bank], the countryside was handsome and open. On the other side, where the King of England would come to Picquigny, the country was also very attractive, except that at the approach to the river opposite Picquigny, there was a causeway, more than two arrow flights long, which had marshes on both sides. For anyone not going there with sincere assurances of his safety, it would have been a very dangerous route. There is no question, as I have said elsewhere, but that the English lack the subtlety in negotiation that the French have; whatever anyone can say, they conduct their affairs very crudely. However, one must have a little patience and not fall into angry debate with them.

The place for the interview having been chosen, orders were given to construct a stout bridge of good size – we furnished the carpenters and the materials. In the middle of the bridge was constructed a strong wooden lattice, like the kind used in making cages for lions. The spaces between the bars were just large enough to permit extending an arm through with ease. For protection against rain there was erected a roof of planks of sufficient size to shelter ten or a dozen persons on each side of the barricade, which spanned the whole width of the bridge so that no one could pass from one side to the other. On the water there was only a single little boat, manned by two rowers, for those who wished to cross the river . . . The bridge and its barricade having been completed, the two kings arrived there the following day, which was [Tuesday] 29 August 1475. The king, who had about eight hundred men of arms with him, was the first to appear. On the King of England's side of the river his whole army was drawn up in battle array; and although we did not think we could see all, there seemed to us to be an amazingly large number of horsemen massed together. What we had on our side could not compare, but then a quarter of our army was not there. It had been arranged that each of the kings would have a dozen men with him, those of highest rank and their most intimate advisers, who had been ordered in advance to station themselves at the barricade. On our side we had four of the King of England's men to keep watch on our proceedings and we had the like number on the King of England's side. . . . It was the king's pleasure to have me dress like him that day. It had long been his custom to have someone dress like him on frequent occasions.

The King of England approached along the causeway I have mentioned, splendidly attended and looking every inch a king. . . . He wore a black velvet cap adorned with large jewelled *fleur-de-lis*. He was a most handsome prince, and tall, but he was beginning to grow fat, and when I had seen him previously he was even handsomer, for I do not remember ever having seen a more handsome man than he was at the time the Earl of Warwick drove him from England [in September 1470].

As he came within four or five feet of the barricade, he removed his cap and half knelt. Our king, who had already leaned against the barricade, did him a similar courtesy, and they then half embraced, their arms thrust through the spaces in the wooden lattice, and the King of England made an even deeper bow. Our king began the conversation by saying, 'Monsieur my cousin, you are most welcome indeed. There is no man in the world I so much long to see as you. Praise be to God that we have met here for this good purpose.' The King of England replied to this greeting in quite good French.

Then the Chancellor of England began to speak. He began with a prophecy – with which the English are never unprovided – which said that at Picquigny an important treaty of peace between France and England would be concluded. Then were brought forward the letters that the king had delivered to the King of England regarding the treaty. The Chancellor asked the king if he had ordered them thus drawn up and if they were satisfactory to him. The king said that they were, as were the letters which had been delivered to him from the King of England.

Thereupon the missal was produced, and each of the kings, extending one hand above it and touching with the other a cross containing a sliver of the True Cross, swore to maintain what they had promised each other – that is, the truce of seven years, including the allies of both sides, and the agreement for the marriage of their children as set forth in the treaty.

After this oath had been taken, our king, who had a ready tongue, said jokingly to the King of England that he would have to come to Paris; our king would offer him entertainments with ladies present and would give him as confessor the Cardinal of Bourbon, who would quickly absolve him of his sins, if he committed any – for King Edward well knew that the cardinal was a *bon compaignon* . . .

As the king was returning to Amiens from the interview, he spoke to me along the road about two aspects of it. He had found the King of England very eager to come to Paris, a fact that had not pleased him. 'He's a very handsome king,' he said.

'He's crazy about women. He could find some clever sweetheart in Paris who would say such nice things to him that she'd make him want to come back.' King Edward's predecessors, he added, had been all too often in Paris and Normandy; he had no desire for his presence on this side of the Channel; but, as long as he stayed on his own side, the king did want him for a good brother and friend.

HENRY VIII
(b. 1491, reigned 1509–1547)

From the Life of Wolsey *by George Cavendish (1554).*

For ten years Cardinal Wolsey enjoyed unparalleled power – a great prince of the church in the medieval tradition. Henry allowed him his influence and his affluence for just as long as it suited him, until Wolsey crossed him in the matter of his proposed marriage to Anne Boleyn. Wolsey died in disgrace on his way to the Tower to face charges of high treason.

Cavendish's account of his master's dealings with Henry give us a glimpse of the early Tudor world with all its ruthless intrigue and king-worship; a marvellously opulent Court, on pleasure bent, where what a man can do with the king's favour may be held against him when that favour is withdrawn. The king's brief and sinister conversation with Cavendish following Wolsey's death leaves no doubt as to the peril of consorting with royalty.

And when it pleased the king's majesty, for his recreation, to resort unto the cardinal's house – as he did divers times in the year, at which time there wanted no preparations or goodly furniture, with viands of the finest sort that might be provided for money or friendship – such pleasures were then devised for the king's comfort and consolation as might be invented or by man's wit imagined. The banquets were set forth with masks and mummeries in so gorgeous a sort and costly manner that it was an heaven to behold. There wanted no dames or damsels meet or apt to dance with the maskers or to garnish the place for the time, with other goodly sports. Then was there all kind of music and harmony set forth, with excellent voices both of men and children. I have seen the king suddenly come in thither in a mask with a dozen other maskers, all in garments like shepherds, made of fine cloth of gold and fine crimson satin paned, and caps of the same, with visors of good proportion, their hairs and beards either of fine gold wires or else of silver, and some being of black silk; having sixteen torch bearers, besides drums and other persons attending upon them, with visors and clothed all in satin of the same colours. And at his coming, and before he came into the hall, ye shall understand that he came by water to the water gate, without any noise. Where, in readiness for his coming, were laid charged many cannon. And at his landing they were all shot off, which made such a rumble in the air that it was like thunder. It made all the noblemen, ladies, and gentlewomen, to muse what it should mean, coming so suddenly; they sitting quietly at a solemn banquet, under this fashion . . .

Then the maskers went first and saluted all the dames as they sat, and then returned to the most worthiest, and there opened a cup full of gold with crowns and other pieces of coin, and set divers pieces to cast at. Thus in this manner they diced with all the ladies and gentlewomen, and to some they lost, and from some they won. And this done, they returned to the cardinal, with great reverence, pouring down all the crowns in the cup, which were about two hundred crowns. 'At all!' quoth the cardinal, and so cast the dice, and won them all at a cast; whereat was great joy made.

Then quoth the cardinal to my Lord Chamberlain, 'I pray you,' quoth he, 'show them that it seems how there should be among them some noble man, whom I suppose to be much more worthy of honour to sit and occupy this place than I. To whom I would most gladly, if I knew him, surrender my place according to my duty.' Then spake my Lord Chamberlain unto them in French, declaring my Lord Cardinal's mind, and they whispering him again in the ear, my Lord Chamberlain said to my Lord Cardinal, 'Sir, they confess,' quoth he, 'that among them there is such a noble personage, who, if your grace can discover him among the others, is contented to disclose himself and to accept your place most worthily.' With that the cardinal, taking a good observation among them, at the last, quoth he, 'Me seems the gentleman with the black beard should be even he.' And with that he arose out of his chair and offered the same to the gentleman in the black beard, with his cap in his hand. The person to whom he offered then his chair was Sir Edward Neville, a comely knight of a goodly personage, that much more resembled the king's person, in that mask, than any other. The king, hearing and perceiving the cardinal so deceived in his estimation and choice, could not forbear laughing; but plucked down his visor, and Master Neville's, and dashed out with such a pleasant countenance and cheer that all the noble personages there assembled, seeing the king to be there amongst them rejoiced very much.

The cardinal at once desired his highness to take the place of state, to whom the king answered that he would go first and shift his apparel. And so he departed, and went straight to my lord's bedchamber, where there was a great fire made and prepared for him; and there he newly apparelled himself with rich and princely garments. And in the time of the king's absence, the dishes of the banquet were clean taken up, and the table was spread again with new and sweet-perfumed cloths; every man sitting still until the king and his maskers came in among them again, every man being newly apparelled. Then the king took his seat under the cloth of state, commanding no man to leave, but sit still as they did before. Then in came a new banquet before the king's majesty, and to all the rest through the tables, wherein, I suppose, were served two hundred dishes or above, of wondrous costly meats and devices, subtly devised. Thus passed they forth the whole night with banqueting, dancing, and other triumphant devices, to the great comfort of the king and pleasant regard of the nobility there assembled.

Henry's conversation with Cavendish after Wolsey's death:

Sir Harry Norris called me, commanding me to come into the king, who stood behind the door in a nightgown of russet velvet, furred with sables. Before whom I kneeled down, being with him there all alone the space of an hour and more, during which time he examined me on divers weighty matters concerning my lord, wishing rather to have lost twenty thousand pounds as long as my lord might have lived. Then he asked me about the fifteen hundred pounds (which Master Kingston made mention of to my lord before his death).

'Sir,' said I, 'I think that I can tell your grace partly where it is.'

'Yea, can you?' quoth the king. 'Then I pray you tell me, and you shall do us much pleasure, nor shall it be unrewarded.'

'Sir,' said I, 'if it please your highness, after the departure from my lord at Scroby of David Vincent, who had then the custody thereof, he left the same with my lord in divers bags sealed with my lord's seal, and my lord delivered the same money in the same bags sealed unto a certain priest (whom I named to the king), safely to keep to his use.'

'Is this true?' quoth the king.

'Yea, sir,' quoth I, 'without all doubt. The priest shall not be able to deny it in my presence, for I was at the delivery thereof.'

'Well then,' quoth the king, 'let me alone, keep this knowledge secret between yourself and me, and let no man be aware thereof. For if I hear any more of it, then I know by whom it is come to knowledge.

An extract from Hall's Chronicle *for the year 1539–40, quoted in* The Private Lives of the Tudor Monarchs *by Christopher Falkus, describes the arrival of Anne of Cleves to meet her new husband. With his eye for rich detail and his delight in pomp and ceremony Hall must have been the Richard Dimbleby of his day:*
When the king knew that she was arrived in her tent, he with all diligence set out through the park. And first issued the king's trumpeters, then the king's officers being sworn of his counsel, next after them followed the gentlemen of the king's privy chamber, some apparelled in coats of velvet embroidered: others had their coats guarded with chains of gold, very rich to behold, which were well horsed and trapped: after them ensued barons, the youngest first, and so Sir William Hollys, knight, Lord Mayor of London, rode with the Lord Parr being

youngest baron. Then followed bishops apparelled in black satin. Then immediately followed the earls, and then Duke Philippe of Bavyer and Count Palantyne of the Rhine, richly apparelled with the livery of the Toysant or Golden Fleece about his neck. Then followed the ambassadors of the French king and the emperor, next followed the Lord Privy Seal, Lord Cromwell, and the Lord Chancellor: then Garter King-of-Arms, and the other officers of arms and the sergeants-at-arms gave their attendance on every side of the lords: which lords for the most part were apparelled in purple velvet, the Lord Marquis Dorset in the same suite bore the king's sword of estate. After him a good distance followed the king's highness mounted on a goodly courser, trapped in rich cloth of gold traversed lattice wise square, all over embroidered with flat gold of damask, pearled on every side of the embroidery, the buckles and pendants were all of fine gold. His person was apparelled in a coat of purple velvet, somewhat made like a frock, all over embroidered with flat gold of damask with small lace mixed between of the same gold and other laces of the same so going traverse wise, that the ground little appeared: about which garment was a rich guard very curiously embroidered, the sleeves and breast were cut, lined with cloth of gold and tied together with great buttons of diamonds, rubies and orient pearl, his sword and swordgirdle adorned with stones and especial emeralds, his night cap garnished with stone, but his bonnet was so rich of jewels that few men could value them. Beside all this he wore in baudrikewise a collar of such ballasts and pearl that few men ever saw the like: and about his person ran ten footmen all richly apparelled in goldsmiths' work. And notwithstanding that this rich apparel and precious jewels were pleasant to the nobles and all other being present to behold, yet his princely countenance, his goodly personage and royal gesture so far exceeded all other creatures being present, that in comparison of his person, all his rich apparel was little esteemed. After him followed his Lord Chamberlain, then came Sir Anthony Browne, master of his horse, a goodly gentleman and a comely personage, well horsed, trapped and richly apparelled leading the king's horse of estate by a long reign of gold, which horse was, trapped in manner like a bard with crimson velvet and satin, all over embroidered with gold after an antique fashion, very curiously wrought. Then followed the pages of honour in coats of rich tinsel and crimson velvet paled, riding on great coursers, all trapped in crimson velvet, embroidered with new devices and knots of gold which were both pleasant and costly to behold. Then followed Sir Anthony Wingfeld, Captain of the Guard, and then the Guard well horsed and in rich coats. In this order the king rode to the last end of the rank where the spears or pensioners stood: and there every person that came with the king placed himself on the one side or the other, the king standing in the midst...

When her grace was advertised of the king's coming, she issued out of her tent being apparelled in a rich gown of cloth of gold, raised made round without any train after the Dutch fashion, and on her head a kall and over that a round bonnet or cap set full of Orient pearl of a very proper fashion, and before that she had a coronet of black velvet, and about her neck she had a portelet set full rich stone which glistened all the field. And at the door of the tent, she mounted on a fair horse richly trapped, with her footmen about her in goldsmiths' work embroidered with the black lion, and on his shoulder a carbuncle gold, and so she marched toward the king: which perceiving her to approach came forward somewhat beyond the cross on Black Heath, and there paused a little in a fair place till she came nearer: then he put off his bonnet and came forward to her, and with most lovely countenance and princely behaviour saluted, welcomed and embraced her to the great rejoicing of the beholders. . . . O what a sight was this to see so goodly a prince and so noble a king to ride with so fair a lady of so goodly a stature and so womanly a countenance, and in especial of so good qualities, I think no creature could see them but his heart rejoiced...

And as they passed they beheld on the wharf how the citizens of London were rowing up and down on the Thames even before them, every craft in his barge garnished with banners, flags, streamers, pensiles and targets, some painted and beaten with the king's arms, some with her grace's arms, and some with the arms of their craft or Mystery. Beside the barges of every craft, there was a barge made like a ship, called the Bachelors barke, decked with cloth of gold, pennons, pensiles and targets in great number, on whom waited a foyst that shot great pieces of artillery. And in every barge was diverse sorts of instruments and children and men singing, which sang and played altogether as the king and the lady passed on thew harf, which sight and noise they much praised and allowed.

When the king and she were within the utter court, they alighted from their horses, and the king lovingly embraced her and kissed her, bidding her welcome to her own, and led her by her left arm through the hall which was furnished beneath the hearth with the king's Guard, and above the hearth with the fifty pensioners with their battle axes, and so brought her up to her privy chamber, where he left her for that time . . .

EDWARD VI
(b. 1537, reigned 1547–1553)

From The Private Lives of the Tudor Monarchs *by Christopher Falkus.*

Edward VI was unique among Tudor sovereigns in that he kept a diary. These brief but fascinating entries are taken from the last year (1552) just before the king died. He was fifteen.

The foresaid challengers came in to the tourney, and the foresaid defendants entered in after[ward] with two more with them – Mr Tyrrell and Mr Robert Hopton – and fought right well, and so the challenge was accomplished. The same night was first a play; after a talk between one that was called Riches, and the other Youth, whether [one] of them was better. After some pretty reasoning there came in six champions of either side:

On Youth's side came:

My Lord Fitzwalter	Sir William Cobham
My Lord Ambrose [Dudley]	Mr Carey
Sir Anthony Browne	Warcopp

On Riches' side:

My Lord FitzWarren	Digby
Sir Robert Stafford	Hopton
Mr Courtney	Hungerford

All these fought two to two at barriers in the hall. Then came in two apparelled like Almains: the Earl of Ormonde and Jacques Granado; and two came in like friars; but the Almains would not suffer them to pass till they had fought. The friars were Mr Drury and Thomas Cobham. After this followed two masques: one of men, another of women. Then a banquet of 120 dishes. This was the end of Christmas.

The Duke of Somerset had his head cut off upon Tower Hill between eight and nine o'clock in the morning.

Sir Ralph Vane was condemned of felony in treason, answering like a ruffian.

Paris arrived with horses and showed how the French king had sent me six curtals, two Turks, a Barbary, two jennets, a stirring horse, and two little mules, and showed them to me.

ELIZABETH I
(b. 1533, reigned 1558–1603)

Elizabeth was undoubtedly one of the best loved of all monarchs. When she succeeded Mary at the age of twenty-five she faced a morose and divided country, but she proved more than a match for it. She was dazzling, energetic, daring, and a consummate politician. She was also woefully indecisive, unnervingly capricious and decidedly moody. One of the most fascinating pictures of her is given by Sir James Melville in his Memoirs *and who was her sister Mary's ambassador. He is not averse to telling a good story and one suspects that some of his more adroit diplomatic utterances may have occurred only in his imagination, but the insights he gives are nevertheless revealing:*

Now I found the Queen of England was determined to treat with my sovereign, first concerning her marriage with the Earl of Leicester, and for that effect she promised to send commissioners unto the Borders. In the meantime I was favourably and familiarly used. For during nine days that I remained at the court, it pleased Her Majesty to confer with me every day, and sometimes thrice in a day, to wit, before noon, after noon and after supper. Sometimes she would say that, seeing she could not meet with the queen her good sister to confer with her familiarly, she should open a good part of her inward mind to me, that I might show it again unto the queen. She told me she was not so offended at the queen's angry letter, as that she seemed so far to disdain the marriage of my Lord of Leicester, which she had caused Mr Randolph to propose to her. . . . Her Majesty was out of all doubt ever to have any children, as being resolved to die a virgin. She said that she was never minded to marry, except she was compelled by the queen her sister's hard behaviour towards her in acting against her advice, as said is. I said, 'Madam, you need not tell me that. I know your stately stomach. You think, if you were married, you would be but Queen of England; and now you are King and Queen both. You may not endure a commander.'

She appeared to be so affectionate to the queen her good sister that she had a great desire to see her. And because their desired meeting could not be so hastily brought to pass, she delighted to look upon Her Majesty's picture. She took me to her bed-chamber and opened a little desk, wherein were divers little pictures wrapt within paper, and their names written with her own hand upon the papers. Upon the first that she took up was written, 'My Lord's picture'. I held the candle, and pressed to see that picture so named. She was loath to let me see it; at length my importunity prevailed for a sight thereof [and found it to be the Earl of Leicester's picture]. I desired that I might have it to carry home to my queen; which she refused, alleging that she had but that one picture of his. I said again that she had the original; for he was at the farthest part of the chamber, speaking with secretary Cecil. Then she took out the queen's picture, and kissed it; and I kissed her hand, for the great love I saw she bore to my mistress. She showed me also a fair ruby, as great as a tennis-ball. I desired that she would either send it, or else my Lord of Leicester's picture, as a token unto the queen. She said, if the queen would follow her counsel, that she would in process of time get them both, and all she had; but in the meantime she was resolved for a token to send her with me a diamond . . .

At divers meetings there would be divers purposes. The queen my sovereign had instructed me to leave matters of gravity sometimes, and cast in merry purposes, lest otherwise I should be tired upon, she being well informed of her sister's natural temper. . . . The Queen of England said she had clothes of every sort; which every day, so long as I was there, she changed. One day she had the English weed, another the French, and another the Italian, and so forth. She asked me which of them became her best. I said, the Italian dress; which pleased her well, for she delighted to shew her golden coloured hair, wearing a caul and bonnet as they do in Italy. Her hair was more reddish than yellow, curled in appearance naturally. Then she entered to discern what colour of hair was reputed best; and whether my queen's hair or her's was best; and which of them two was fairest. I answered that the fairness of them both was not their worst faults. But she was earnest with me to declare which of them I thought fairest. I said she was the fairest queen in England and ours the fairest queen in Scotland. Yet she was earnest. I answered they were both the fairest ladies of their courts and that Her Majesty was whiter, but our queen was very lovely. She enquired which of them was of highest stature. I said, our queen. Then, saith she, she is too high and that herself was neither too high nor too low. Then she asked what kind of exercises she used. I answered that [when] I was despatched out of Scotland, the queen was lately come from the highland hunting; that when she had leisure from the affairs of her country she read upon good books, the histories of diverse countries, and sometimes would play upon the lute and virginals. She asked if she played well. I said, reasonably for a queen . . .

I was earnest to be despatched, but she said I was weary sooner of her company than she was of mine. I told Her Majesty that though I had no reason of being weary, it was time to return. But I was stayed two days longer, till I might see her dance, as I was informed. Which being done, she enquired of me whether she or my queen danced best. I answered that the queen danced not so high and disposedly as she did . . .

In Brief Lives *John Aubrey recounts two delightful snippets of gossip:*
Queen Elizabeth loved to have all the servants of her court proper men, and (as beforesaid Sir W.R.'s graceful presence was no mean recommendation to him), I think his first preferment at court was captain of her majesty's guard. There came a country gentleman (or sufficient yeoman) up to town, who had several sons, but one an extraordinary proper handsome fellow, whom he did hope to have preferred to be a yeoman of the guard. The father (a goodly man himself) comes to Sir Walter Raleigh a stranger to him, and told him that he had brought up a boy that he would desire (having many children) should be one of her majesty's guard. Quoth Sir Walter Raleigh, 'Had you spoken for yourself, I should readily have granted your desire, for your person deserves it, but I put in no boys.' Said the father, 'Boy, come in.' The son enters, about 18 or 19, but such a goodly proper young fellow, as Sir Walter Raleigh had not seen the like – he was the tallest of all the guard. Sir Walter swears him immediately; and ordered him to carry up the first dish at dinner, where the queen beheld him with admiration, as if a beautiful young giant had stalked with the service.

This Earl of Oxford, Edward de Vere, making of his low obeisance to Queen Elizabeth, happened to fart, at which he was so abashed that he went to travel [for] seven years. On his return the queen welcomed him home and said, 'My lord, I had forgotten the fart.'

In a letter to Mr Robert Markham, written in 1606 and quoted in The Private Lives of the Tudor Monarchs, *Sir John Harington, the queen's favourite godson, lovingly and shrewdly portrays her in her old age:*
Sir Christopher Hatton was wont to say, 'The queen did fish for men's souls, and had so sweet a bait, that no one could escape her network'. In truth, I am sure her speech was such, as none could refuse to take delight in when forwardness did

not stand in the way. I have seen her smile, sooth with great semblance of good liking to all around, and cause every one to open his most inward thought to her; when, on a sudden, she would ponder in private on what had passed, write down all their opinions, draw them out as occasion required, and sometime disprove to their faces what had been delivered a month before. Hence she knew one's part, and by thus fishing, as Hatton said, she caught many poor fish, who little knew what snare was laid for them.

I will now tell you more of her majesty's discretion and wonder working to those about her, touching their minds and opinions. She did oft ask the ladies around her chamber if they loved to think of marriage? And the wise ones did conceal well their liking hereto; as knowing the queen's judgment in this matter. Sir Matthew Arundel's fair cousin, not knowing so deeply as her fellows, was asked one day hereof, and simply said – 'She had thought much about marriage, if her father did consent to the man she loved' – 'You seem honest, i'faith', said the queen; 'I will sue for you to your father' – The damsel was not displeased hereat; and, when Sir Robert came to court the queen asked him hereon, and pressed his consenting, if the match was discreet. Sir Robert, much astounded at this news, said – 'He never heard his daughter had liking to any man, and wanted to gain knowledge of her affection; but would give free consent to what was most pleasing to her Highness' will and advice.' – 'Then I will do the rest;' saith the queen. The lady was called in, and the queen told her father had given his free consent. 'Then', replied the lady, 'I shall be happy, and please your grace.' – 'So thou shalt; but not to be a fool and marry. I have his consent given to me, and I vow thou shalt never get it into thy possession: so, go to thy business. I see thou art a bold one, to own thy foolishness so readily.'

I could relate many pleasant tales of her majesty's outwitting the wittiest ones; for few knew how to aim their shaft against her cunning. We did all love her, for she said she loved us, and much wisdom she showed in this matter. She did well temper herself towards all at home, and put at variance those abroad; by which means she had more quit than her neighbours. I need not praise her frugality; but I will tell a story that fell out when I was a boy. She did love a rich clothing, but often chide those that bought more finery than became their state. It happened that Lady M. Howard was possessed of a rich border, powdered with gold and pearl, and a velvet suit belonging thereto, which moved many to envy; nor did it please the queen, who thought it exceeded her own. One day the queen did send privately, and got the lady's rich vesture, which she put on herself, and came forth the chamber among the ladies; the kirtle and border was far too short for her majesty's height; and she asked every one, 'How they liked her new-fancied suit'? At length, she asked the owner herself, 'If it was not made too short and ill-becoming'? which the poor lady did presently consent to. 'Why then, if it become not me, as being too short, I am minded it shall never become thee, as being too fine; so it fitteth neither well.' This sharp rebuke abashed the lady, and she never adorned her herewith any more. I believe the vestment was laid up till after the queen's death.

As I did bear so much love toward her majesty, I know not well how to stop my tales of her virtues, and sometimes her faults, for *nemo nascitur sine* – saith the poet; but even her errors did seem great marks of surprising endowments. When she smiled, it was a pure sunshine, that every one did choose to bask in, if they could; but anon came a storm from a sudden gathering of clouds, and the thunder fell in wondrous manner on all alike.

JAMES I
(b. 1566, reigned 1603–1625)

While Elizabeth I was on the whole affectionately served by her various biographers, James was less lucky. Even Melville's description of the baptism of James's first son has a ludicrous aspect to it, and Sir John Harington's jaundiced account of an entertainment in honour of Christian IV of Denmark is downright farcical. Francis Bacon fared little better when he tried to arrange a spectacular on the Thames. There is a touch of the 'damp squib' about all these royal occasions.

From John Aubrey's Brief Lives*:*
It was a most stately sight, the glory of that reception of his majesty, where the nobility and gentry were in exceeding rich equipage, having enjoyed a long peace under the most excellent of queens; and the company was so exceeding numerous that their obedience [respect] carried a secret dread with it. King James did not inwardly like it, and with an inward envy said that he doubted not but he should have been able on his own strength to have dealt with them, and get his right. Said Sir Walter Raleigh to him 'Would to God that had been put to trial.' 'Why do you wish that?' said the king. – 'Because,' said Sir Walter, 'that then you would have known your friends from your foes.' But that reason of Sir Walter was never forgotten nor forgiven.

From The Memoirs of Sir James Melville of Halhill*:*
Now the prince being born at Stirling the [19 February 1594] His Majesty thought fit to send ambassadors to England, Denmark France and Flanders, to require their ambassadors to be sent to the baptism of the prince his first-born son. The council were commanded to nominate such as were meetest to be sent on that message; as they did. Yet such as procured to be sent obtained the commission, although some of them were unmeet for that errand, as Sir William Keith; he could neither speak Latin, French nor Flemish. The laird of Easter Wemyss procured to carry the commission to France, and also to England, because he was to go thither about his own affairs, being the King of France's servant. But Mr Peter Young sped best, who was sent to Denmark, and to the Dukes of Mecklenburg and Brunswick; for he got three fair chains. But the King of France nor the Queen of England gave nothing; which their duty would have caused them to do, if ambassadors had been sent to them express. Neither sent the King [of France] any ambassador here at that time. The Queen of England was at first minded to do the same, till she was advertised by her ambassador in France that the king would send none. Then very late she sent the Earl of Sussex, to let us think that she would ever be a ready friend, when France would refuse and lie back. On the other part, the Dukes of Mecklenburg and

Brunswick were discontent that they were so far slighted, as not to have a man sent express to each of them. A special day was appointed for solemnizing the said baptism. The ambassadors of Denmark and Dutchland arrived almost together. His Majesty had sent for me of before to be there at their landing, to receive them and to entertain them. But the ambassadors of Mecklenburg and Brunswick would not ride out of Leith in company with the Danish ambassador, when they were convoyed up to Edinburgh, but would have a convoy apart.

A few days after them arrived the ambassadors of the estates of the Low Countries, to wit, Monsieur de Brederod and Monsieur Folk. A little before the landing of the said ambassadors, the day of the baptism was delayed, because there was no word of an ambassador from France or England, and the king's chapel in the castle of Stirling, which was cast down, to be built again in a better form, was not yet completed: so that the ambassadors were ordained to remain in Edinburgh till all might be put in good order.

Now being in doubt of the English ambassador's coming, the ceremony was to be solemnized without longer delay. In the meantime, there came word that the Earl of Sussex was upon his journey toward Scotland, for the queen his mistress, on whom the action stayed. The day of the solemnity, there was great business for their honours and seats. That being agreed, there was an empty chair set before the rest for the King of France's ambassador. The order of the banquet and triumph I leave to others to set out.

Sir John Harington, from Music at Court *by Christopher Hogwood:*

One day a great feast was held, and after dinner the representation of Solomon his Temple and the coming of the Queen of Sheba was made, or, as I may better say, was meant to have been made, before their Majesties, by device of the Earl of Salisbury and others. – But alas! as all earthly thinges do fail to poor mortals in enjoyment, so did prove our presentment hereof. The Lady who did play the Queens part did carry most precious gifts to both their Majesties; but forgetting the steppes arising to the canopy, overset her caskets into his

Danish Majesties lap, and fell at his feet, tho I rather think it was in his face. Much was the hurry and confusion; cloths and napkins were at hand to make all clean. His Majesty then got up and woud dance with the Queen of Sheba; but he fell down and humbled himself before her, and was carried to an inner chamber and laid on a bed of state; which was not a little defiled with the presents of the Queen which had been bestowed on his garments; such as wine, cream, jelly, beverage, cakes, spices, and other good matters. The entertainment and shew went forward and most of the presenters went backward, or fell down, wine did so occupy their upper chambers. Now did appear in rich dress, Hope, Faith, and Charity: Hope did assay to speak, but wine rendered her endeavours so feeble that she withdrew, and hoped the King would excuse her brevity. Faith was then all alone, for I am certain she was not joyned with good works; and left the Court in a staggering condition. Charity came to the Kings feet, and seemed to cover the multitude of sins her sisters had committed: In some sorte she made obeysance and brought giftes, but said she would return home again, as there was no gift which Heaven had not already given his Majesty; she then returned to Hope and Faith, who were both sick and spewing in the lower hall.

Next came *Victory*, in bright armour, and presented a rich sword to the King, who did not accept it, but put it by with his hand; and, by a strange medley of versification, did endeavour to make suit to the King; but Victory did not tryumph for long, for, after much lamentable utterance, she was led away like a silly captive, and laid to sleep in the outer steps of the antichamber. Now did Peace make entry, and strive to get foremoste to the King; but I grieve to tell how great wrath she did discover unto those of her attendants, and, much contrary to her own semblance, most rudely made war with her olive brance, and laid on the pates of those who did oppose her coming. I have much marvelled at these strange pageantries, and they do bring to my remembrance what passed of this sort in our Queens days; of which I was sometime an humble presenter and assistant; but I neer did see such lack of good order, discretion, and sobreity, as I have now done . . .

In Music at Court *Sir John Chamberlain describes the masque in honour of the marriage of James's daughter Elizabeth to Frederick, Elector Palatine:*

Their shew by water was very gallant by reason of infinite store of lights very curiously set and placed; and many boats and barges with devices of light of lamps with three peals of ordnance, one at their taking water, another in the Temple-garden, and the last at their landing; which passage by water cost them better than £300. They were received at the Privy Stairs; a great expectation there was that they should every way excel their competitors that went before them, both in devise, daintiness of apparel, and, above all, in dancing, wherein they are held excellent, and esteemed the properer men. But by what ill planet it fell out, I know not; they came home as they went without doing anything; the reason whereof I cannot yet learn thoroughly, but only that the Hall was so full that it was not possible to avoid it, or make room for them; besides that most of the Ladies were in the Galleries to see them land, and could not get in. But the worst of all was, that the King was so wearied and sleepy with setting up almost two whole nights before, that he had no edge to it. Whereupon, Sir Francis Bacon ventured to entreat his Majesty, that by this disgrace he would not as it were bury them quick; and I hear the King should answer, that then they must bury him quick, for he could last no longer; but withall gave them very good words, and appointed them to come again on Saturday. But the grace of the Mask was quite gone, when their apparel hath been already showed, and their devices vented, so that how it will fall out God knows; for they are much discouraged and out of countenance, and the world says it comes to pass after the old proverb, 'the properer men the worse luck'.

The king made good his bad manners, however, by commending the performance when it eventually took place, and the music was judged very effective:

The Statues enter, and at their coming, the musick changed from violins to hautboys, cornets, &c. and the air of the musick was utterly turned into a soft time, with drawing notes, excellently expressing their natures. The musick was extremely well-fitted, having such a spirit of country jollity as can hardly be imagined; but the perpetual laughter and applause was above the musick.

James so enjoyed the statue scene that at the end of the performance he called for it again; 'but one of the Statues by that time was undressed'.

CHARLES I

(b. 1600, reigned 1625–1649)

Charles had a strong and sincere belief in the Divine Right of Kings which led him to quarrel with parliament very early in his reign. Some of England's most powerful and uncompromising figures objected strongly to his concept of monarchy, his advisors, his religion and his queen, though it was more than fifteen years before their grievances precipitated civil war. When Charles was finally brought to trial he conducted himself with grace and dignity, demonstrating that even an execution can be a royal occasion.

John Evelyn, with Pepys one of the two great English diarists, records the general uncertainty of 1640:
On April the 11th I went to London to see the solemnity of His Majesty's riding in state through the City, to the Short Parliament, which began on the 13th following. It was a very glorious and magnificent sight – the king circled with his royal diadem and the affections of his people . . .

London, and especially the Court, were at this period in frequent disorders, and great insolencies were committed by the abused, and too happy, city. In particular, the Bishop of Canterbury's palace at Lambeth was assaulted by a rude rabble from Southwark, my Lord Chamberlain imprisoned, and many scandalous libels and invectives were scattered about the streets – to the reproach of government and the fermentation of our later distractions.

On October 30th, I saw his Majesty ride in pomp and a kind of ovation – with all the marks of an happy peace, and restored to the affections of his people – being conducted through

London with a most splendid cavalcade. But in November following, and upon the *third* (a day never to be mentioned without a curse) he was conducted to that long, ungrateful, foolish and fatal Parliament, the beginning of all our sorrows for twenty years after, and the end of the most happy monarch in the world.

Edward Hyde, Earl of Clarendon, in The History of the Great Rebellion, *evokes the Civil War battlefields of 1642:*
After a very cold night spent in the field, without any refreshment of victual or provision for the soldiers (for the country was so disaffected that it not only not sent in provisions, but many soldiers who straggled into the villages for relief were knocked in the head by the common people) the king found his troops very thin. And though by conference with the officers he might reasonably conclude that there were not many slain in the battle, yet a third part of his foot were not upon the place, and of the horse many were missing, and they that were in the field were so tired with duty and weakened with want of meat, and shrunk up with the cruel cold of the night (for it was a terrible frost, and there was not shelter of either tree or hedge), that though they had reason to believe (by the standing still of the enemy whilst a small part of the king's horse in the morning took away four pieces of their cannon very near them) that any offer towards a charge, or but marching towards them, would have made a very notable impression on them; yet there was so visible an averseness from it in most officers as well as soldiers that the king thought not fit to make the attempt. He contented himself to keep his men in order, the body of horse facing the enemy upon the field where they had fought.

Towards noon the king resolved to try that expedient which was prepared for the day before, and sent Sir William le Neve, Clarenceux king-at-arms, with his proclamation of pardon to such as would lay down arms, to the enemy. He believed (though he expected then little benefit by the proclamation) that he should by that means receive some advertisement of the condition of the army, and what prisoners they had taken, for many persons of command and quality were wanting. He gave him order likewise to desire to speak with the Earl of

Lindsey, who was known to be in their hands. Before Sir William came to the army he was received by the outguards, and conducted with strictness, that he might say or publish nothing amongst the soldiers, to the Earl of Essex. When he offered to read the proclamation aloud, and to deliver the effect of it, that he might be heard by those who were present, the earl rebuked him with some roughness, and charged him as he loved his life not to presume to speak a word to the soldiers, and after some few questions sent him presently back, well guarded, through the army, without any answer at all.

From John Evelyn's Diary*:*
30 January 1649:
The villainy of the rebels now proceeded so far that they tried, condemned, and, on the 30th of this month, murdered our excellent King. I was struck with such horror that I kept the day of his Martyrdom a fast, and would not be present at that execrable wickedness, receiving a sad account of it from my brother George.

John Rushworth's account of the execution, from The Trial of Charles I*:*
The scaffold was hung round with black, and the floor covered with black, and the axe and block laid in the middle of the scaffold. There were divers companies of Foot and Horse on every side of the scaffold, and the multitudes of people that came to be spectators were very great. The King making a pass upon the scaffold, looked very earnestly on the block, and asked Colonel Hacker if there were no higher, and then spoke thus, directing his speech to the gentlemen on the scaffold.

King 'I shall be very little heard of any body here, I shall therefore speak a word unto you here. Indeed I could hold my peace very well, if I did not think that holding my peace would make some men think that I did submit to the guilt, as well as to the punishment. But I think it is my duty to God first, and to my Country, for to clear myself both as an honest man, a good king, and a good christian. I shall begin first with my innocence. In troth, I think it not very needful for me to insist long upon this, for all the world knows I never did begin the war with the two Houses of Parliament, and I call God to witness (to whom I must shortly make an account) that I never did intend to incroach upon their privileges. They began upon me. It is the militia they began upon, they confest that the Militia was mine, but they thought it fit to have it from me. And to be short, if anybody will look but to the dates of the commissions, their commissions and mine, and likewise to the declarations, will see clearly that they began these unhappy troubles, not I. So that as to the guilt of these enormous Crimes that are laid against me, I hope in God, that God will clear me of it.

. . . As for the King, the Laws of the Land will clearly instruct you for that, therefore because it concerns my own particular, I only give you a touch of it. For the People, and truly I desire their liberty and freedom, as much as anybody whomsoever, but I must tell you, that their liberty and freedom consist in having of Government, those laws by which their life and their goods may be most their own. . . . A subject and a sovereign are clean different things, and therefore, until they do that, I mean, that you do put the people in that liberty as I say, certainly they will never enjoy themselves. Sirs, it was for this that now I am come here. If I would have given way to an arbitrary way, for to have all laws changed according to the Power of the Sword, I needed not to have come here, and therefore I tell you, (and I pray God it be not laid to your Charge), that I am the Martyr of the people. In troth, Sirs, I shall not hold you much longer, for I will only say this to you, . . . that I die a christian according to the profession of the Church of England as I found it left me by my Father, and this honest man (*meaning the Bishop*) I think will witness it.' Then turning to the Officers, said: 'Sirs, excuse me for this same, I have a good cause, and I have a gracious God, I will say no more.' Then turning to Colonel Hacker he said, 'Take care that they do not put me to pain, and Sir, this and it please you – ' But then a gentleman coming near the axe, the King said, 'Take heed of the Axe, pray take heed of the Axe.' Then the King speaking to the Executioner, said, 'I shall say but very short prayers, and then thrust out my hands.' Then the King called to Dr Juxon for his nightcap, and having put it on, he said to the Executioner, 'Does my hair trouble you.' Who desired him to put it all under his cap, which the King did accordingly by the help of the Executioner and the Bishop. Then the King turning to Dr Juxon, said, 'I have a good cause and a gracious God on my side.'

Dr Juxon 'There is but one stage more. This stage is turbulent and troublesome, it is a short one. But you may consider it will soon carry you a very great way, it will carry you from earth to heaven, and there you shall find to your great joy the prize. You haste to a crown of glory.'

The King 'I go from a corruptible to an incorruptible Crown, where no disturbance can be.'

Dr Juxon 'You are exchanged from a temporal to an eternal Crown, a good exchange.'

Then the King took off his cloak and his George, giving his George to Dr Juxon, saying, 'Remember,' (it is thought for the Prince) and some other small ceremonies [were] past. After which the King stooping down, laid his neck upon the block. And after a little pause, stretching forth his hands, the Executioner at one blow severed his head from his body.

CHARLES II
(b. 1630, reigned 1660–1685)

These extracts from John Evelyn's diary cover many royal occasions, including Charles's triumphal entry into London, the coronation, the queen's birthday and the king's death – which was as lacking in privacy as his life. Evelyn sums him up affectionately: 'An excellent prince, doubtless, had he been less addicted to women ...'

1660
February the 6th. This day was His Majesty proclaimed in London.

The 29th. This day, after a sad and long exile, and after calamitous suffering of both the king and church for seventeen years, His Majesty King Charles II came to London: this day was also his birthday. He came with a triumph of over twenty thousand horse and foot brandishing their swords and shouting with unexpressable joy. The ways were strewn with flowers, the bells were ringing, the streets were hung with tapestry, and the fountains were running wine. The mayor, aldermen, and all the companies, in their chains of gold, liveries, and banners, were present; also, the lords and nobles. Everybody was clad in cloth of silver, gold, and velvet; the windows and balconies were all set with ladies, trumpets and music, and myriads of people flocked the streets as far as Rochester, so that they took seven hours to pass through the city – even from two in the afternoon till nine at night. I stood in the Strand and beheld it and blessed God. And all this was done without one drop of blood shed and by that very army which had rebelled against him.

June: The greediness of all sorts of men, women and children to see His Majesty and kiss his hands – insomuch that he had scarcely leisure to eat for some days – was indeed intolerable as well as unexpressable. They came from all parts of the nation: and the king, for his part, was willing to give them that satisfaction and would have none kept out, but gave free access to all sorts of people . . .

July the 6th. According to custom, His Majesty first began to touch for the King's Evil. Thus, His Majesty sitting under his cloth of state in the Banqueting House, the surgeons cause the sick to be brought, or led up, to the throne; who, kneeling, the King strokes their faces or cheeks with both his hands at once; at which instant, a chaplain in his formalities says 'He put his hands upon them, and he healed them' – this is said to every one in particular. When they have all been touched, they come up again in the same order, and the other chaplain, kneeling, and having the gold Angel, or touch piece, strung on white ribbon on his arm, delivers them one by one to His Majesty, who puts them about the neck of the touched as they pass, whilst the first chaplain repeats 'That is the true light who came into the world'. Then follows an Epistle (as, at first, a Gospel) and the prayers for the sick, taken from the Liturgy, with some alteration. Lastly comes the Blessing: and then the Lord Chamberlain and the Comptroller of the Household bring basin, ewer, and towel, for His Majesty to wash . . .

1661

On April the 23rd was the Coronation of His Majesty King Charles the Second in the Abbey Church of Westminster, at all of which I was present. A magnificent train on horseback, as rich as embroidery, velvet, cloth of gold, silk, and jewels, could make them and their prancing horses, proceeded through streets strewn with flowers. The houses were hung with rich tapestry, the windows and balconies were full of ladies, the London militia lined the ways, and the several Companies, with their banners and loud music, were ranked in their orders. Fountains were running wine, bells were ringing, and speeches were made at the several triumphal arches. At that of the Temple Bar, near which I stood, the Lord Mayor was received by the Bailiff of Westminster who, in a scarlet robe, made a speech. Thence, with joyful acclamation, His Majesty passed to Whitehall. There were bonfires that night, and the next day, being St George's Day, he went by water to Westminster Abbey. When His Majesty was entered, the dean and prebends brought all the Regalia, and delivered it to several noblemen to bear before the king – who met them at the West door of the church – to the Choir, while an anthem was sung. Then came the peers in their robes, with their coronets in their hands, till His Majesty was placed on a throne elevated before the altar. The Archbishop of Canterbury being sick, the Bishop of London then went to every side of the throne to present the king to the people, asking if they would have him for their king and do him homage: at which they four times shouted GOD SAVE KING CHARLES THE SECOND. Then an anthem was sung, and His Majesty, attended by three bishops, went up to the altar and offered a pall and a pound of gold. Then sat he down in another chair during the sermon, which was preached by Dr Morley, then Bishop of Worcester. After the sermon, the king took his oath before the altar to maintain the religion, Magna Carta, and the Laws of the Land: next, the hymn *Veni Sanctus Spiritus*; then the Litany, by two bishops.

Now the Lord Archbishop of Canterbury, who was present though much indisposed and weak, said 'Lift up your hearts'. The king rose up and put off his robes and upper garments, revealing a waistcoat which was opened in divers places so that the archbishop might commodiously anoint him: first, on the palms of his hands; then was sung an anthem and a prayer: and then on his breast, between his shoulders, at the bending of both his arms, and the crown of his head; with apposite hymns and prayers at each anointing. Next, the waistcoat was closed and buttoned up, which was done by the dean. Then the archbishop placed the Crown Imperial on the altar, prayed over it, and set it on His Majesty's head: at which all the peers put on their coronets, and anthems and rare music were played with lutes, viols, trumpets, organs, voices, etc. Now the archbishop put a ring on His Majesty's finger, and the king offered his sword on the altar, which, being redeemed, was drawn and borne before him. Then the archbishop delivered him the sceptre with the dove in one hand, and the sceptre with the orb in the other. Then, the king kneeling, the archbishop pronounced the blessing. Next the king ascended his royal throne and, while the *Te Deum* was being sung, all the peers did their homage by touching his crown, the archbishop and the rest of the bishops first kissing the king. Then he received the Holy Sacrament, and so disrobed, yet with the Crown Imperial on his head. And then, accompanied by all the nobility in the former order, he went on foot upon blue cloth which was spread from the west door of the Abbey to Westminster Stairs, where he took water in a triumphal barge to Whitehall, where there was extraordinary feasting . . .

On the 13th of September, to London. On the 14th I presented my *Fumifugium: or the inconvenience of the air and smoke of London dissipated*, which was dedicated to His Majesty – who was pleased I should publish it by his special command; for he was much pleased with it . . .

October the 1st. I sailed this morning with His Majesty on the *Mary*, one of his yachts, or pleasure boats. These vessels were unknown amongst us until the Dutch East India Company presented this curious piece to the king; but they are very excellent sailing vessels. There was a wager between his other new pleasure boat, the *Catharine*, and the *Anne*, one of the Duke of York's. The wager was for £100: the race, from Greenwich to Gravesend and back. The king lost it going, for the wind was contrary, but saved his stakes coming back. I dined in his yacht, where we all ate together with His Majesty. In this passage, His Majesty was pleased to discourse with me about my book, inveighing against the nuisance of the smoke of London and proposing expedients how, by removing those particulars I mentioned, it might be reformed.

1684

November the 15th. Being the queen's birthday, there were such fireworks upon the Thames before Whitehall – with pageants of castles, forts, and other devices of revolving wheels, serpents, and the king's and queen's arms and mottoes all represented in fire – as had not been seen in any age remembered here. But that which was most remarkable was the several fires and skirmishes in the very water, which actually moved a long way, burning under the water and now and then appearing above it, giving reports like muskets and cannon, with grenades and innumerable other devices. It is said this sole triumph cost £1500. It was concluded with a ball, where all the young ladies and gallants danced in the Great Hall, and the court had not been seen so brave and rich in apparel since His Majesty's Restoration.

1685

January the 25th. I saw this evening such a scene of profuse gaming and luxurious dallying and prophaneness – the king in the midst of his three concubines – as I had never seen before.

February the 4th. I went to London, hearing His Majesty had been the Monday before surprised in his bedchamber with an apoplectical fit. If, by God's providence, Dr King – that excellent surgeon as well as physician – had not been accidentally present with his lancet in his pocket, His Majesty had certainly died that moment. This rescued His Majesty for that instant, but it proved only a reprieve for a little time. He still complained, and was relapsing and often fainting, and sometimes in epileptical symptoms, till Wednesday – for which he was cupped, let blood again in both jugularies, and had both vomit and purges. These so relieved him that on the Thursday hopes of recovery were signified in the Public Gazette. But that day, about noon, the physicians conjectured him somewhat feverish. . . . After some conflicts, the physicians despairing of him, he gave up the ghost at half an hour after eleven in the morning, being the sixth of February in the thirty-seventh year of his reign and fifty-fifth of his age.

'Tis not to be expressed, the tears and sorrow of court, city, and country. Those who assisted His Majesty's devotion were the Archbishop of Canterbury and the Bishops of London, Durham and Ely, but, more especially, the Bishop of Bath and Wells. It is said they exceedingly urged the receiving of the Holy Sacrament, but that His Majesty told them he would consider of it, which he did so long till it was too late. Others whisper that, the bishops being bid withdraw some time the night before, Huddleston, the priest, had presumed to administer the popish offices. I hope it is not true. He gave his breeches and keys to the duke, who was almost continually kneeling by his bedside, and in tears. He also recommended to him the care of his natural children, all except the Duke of Monmouth, now in Holland and in his displeasure. He entreated the queen to pardon him (nor without cause) who, a little before, had sent a bishop to excuse her not more frequently visiting him, in regard to her excessive grief, and, withal, that His Majesty would forgive it if at any time she had offended him. He spake to the duke to be kind to his concubines, the Duchess of Cleveland and, especially, Portsmouth, and that Nelly might not starve. But I do not hear he said anything of the church or his people, now falling under the government of a prince suspected for his religion after, for above a hundred years, the church and nation had been departed from Rome.

Thus died King Charles II, of a vigorous and robust constitution, and in all appearance capable of a longer life. A prince of many virtues and many great imperfections, he was debonair, easy of access, and not bloody or cruel. His countenance was fierce, and his voice great. He was proper of person, and every motion became him. He was a lover of the sea, and skilful in shipping, not affecting other studies, yet he had a laboratory and knew of many empirical medicines and the easier mechanical mathematics. He loved planting and building, and brought in a politer way of living, which passed to luxury and intolerable expense. He had a particular talent in telling stories and facetious passages – of which he had innumerable – which made some buffoons and vicious wretches too familiar and presumptuous, not worthy the favours they abused. He took delight to have a number of little spaniels follow him and lie in his bedchamber, where oftentimes he suffered the bitches to puppy and give suck, which rendered it very offensive and indeed made the whole court nasty and stinking. An excellent prince, doubtless, had he been less addicted to women.

GEORGE I
(b. 1660, reigned 1714–1727)

The accession of George I by Act of Parliament marked a switch from an Anglo-Scottish monarchy to an Anglo-German line which has not been interrupted since. He never learned English and spent little time in his new kingdom; however his reunion with his former Court Composer, Handel, did give us The Water Music, *and this endearing description of a court picnic . . . from* Music at Court *by Christopher Hogwood:*

About eight in the evening the King repaired to His barge, into which were admitted the Duchess of Bolton, Countess Godolphin, Mad. de Kilmanseck, Mrs Were and the Earl of Orkney, the Gentleman of the Bedchamber in Waiting. Next to the King's barge was that of the musicians, about 50 in number, who played on all kinds of instruments, to wit trumpets, horns, hautboys, bassoons, German flutes, French flutes, violins and basses; but there were no singers, The music had been composed specially by the famous Handel, a native of Halle, and His Majesty's principal Court Composer. His Majesty approved of it so greatly that he caused it to be repeated three times in all, although each performance lasted an hour – namely twice before and once after supper. The evening was all that could be desired for the festivity, the number of barges and above all of boats filled with people desirous of hearing was beyond counting. In order to make this entertainment the more exquisite, Mad. de Kilmanseck had arranged a choice supper in the late Lord Ranelagh's villa at Chelsea on the river, where the king went at one in the morning. He left at three o'clock and returned to St James' about half past four. The concert cost Baron Kilmanseck £150 for the musicians alone.

THE PRINCE REGENT, GEORGE IV
(b. 1762, reigned 1820–1830)

'As a young prince he was extravagant, witty and undisciplined in taste and in love; as an old king he was an embarrassing, corpulent voluptuary bursting out of his clothes.' He outraged everyone by marrying a Roman Catholic widow, Mrs Fitzherbert; and was later induced to marry Caroline of Brunswick, a gauche, ungainly Protestant princess whom he disliked intensely, in order to persuade Parliament to take responsibility for his massive debts. History relates that he had to drink himself almost into insensibility before the wedding, and within a year he had banished his graceless consort from his bed, his presence and her child. It is hardly surprising that his reign should have thrown up one of our most entertaining gossips in Creevey, a most accomplished raconteur in Gronow, and that brazenly attractive hunter in the dandy jungle, Miss Harriet Wilson. It is also hardly surprising that any attempt at ritual splendour was reduced to farce. Even the fiercely partisan Nightingale cannot make his account of the injured Queen Caroline's attempt to be present at her own coronation anything but hilarious.

LIFE AT THE PAVILION

From The Creevey Papers *by Thomas Creevey:*
1805
I suppose the courts or houses of princes are all alike in one thing, viz., that in attending them you lose your liberty. After one month was gone by, you fell naturally and of course into

the ranks, and had to reserve your observations till you were asked for them. These royal invitations are by no means calculated to reconcile one to a court. To be sent for half an hour before dinner, or perhaps in the middle of one's own, was a little too humiliating to be very agreeable . . .

I had heard a great deal of the prince's drinking, but, during the time that I speak of, I never saw him the least drunk but once, and I was myself pretty much the occasion of it. We were dining at the Pavilion, and poor Fonblanque, a dolorous fop of a lawyer, and a member of parliament too, was one of the guests. After drinking some wine, I could not resist having some jokes at Fonblanque's expense, which the prince encouraged greatly. I went on and invented stories about speeches Fonblanque had made in parliament, which were so pathetic as to have affected his audience to tears, all of which inventions of mine Fonblanque denied to be true with such overpowering gravity that the prince said he should die of it if I did not stop . . . In the evening, at about ten or eleven o'clock, he said he would go to the ball at the castle, and said I should go with him. So I went in his coach, and he entered the room with his arm through mine, everybody standing and getting upon benches to see him. He was certainly tipsey, and so, of course, was I, but not much, for I well remember his taking me up to Mrs Creevey and her daughters, and telling them he had never spent a pleasanter day in his life, and that 'Creevey had been very great'. He used to drink a great quantity of wine at dinner, and was very fond of making any newcomer drunk by drinking wine with him very frequently, always recommending his strongest wines, and at last some remarkable strong old brandy which he called Diabolino.

It used to be the Duke of Norfolk's custom to come over every year from Arundel to pay his respects to the prince and to stay two days at Brighton, both of which he always dined at the Pavilion. In the year 1804, upon this annual visit, the prince had drunk so much as to be made very seriously ill by it, so that in 1805 (the year I was there) when the duke came, Mrs Fitzherbert, who was always the prince's best friend, was very much afraid of his being again made ill, and she persuaded the prince to adopt different stratagems to avoid drinking with the duke. I dined there on both days, and letters were brought in each day after dinner to the prince, which he affected to consider of great importance, and so went out to answer them, while the Duke of Clarence went on drinking with the Duke of Norfolk. But on the second day this joke was carried too far, and in the evening the Duke of Norfolk showed he was affronted. The prince took me aside and said – 'Stay after everyone is gone tonight. The Jockey's got sulky, and I must give him a broiled bone to get him in good humour again.' So of course I stayed, and about one o'clock the Prince of Wales and Duke of Clarence, the Duke of Norfolk and myself sat down to a supper of broiled bones, the result of which was, having fallen asleep myself, I was awoke by the sound of the Duke of Norfolk's snoring. I found the Prince of Wales and the Duke of Clarence in a very animated discussion as to the particular shape and make of the wig worn by George II . . .

Mrs Creevey to Creevey:

Brighton 29 October 1805

Oh, this wicked Pavillion! we were there till ½ past one this morng., and it has kept me in bed with the headache till 12 to-day . . .

1811

Brighton, Oct. 30th. – The Prince Regent came here last night with the Duke of Cumberland and Lord Yarmouth. Everybody has been writing their names at the Pavilion this morning, but I don't hear of anybody dining there to-day. . . . I presume we shall be asked there, altho' I went to town on purpose to vote against his appointment of his brother the Duke of York to the Commandership-in-Chief of the army.

Oct. 31st. – We have got an invitation from the Regent for to-night and are going. I learn from Sir Philip Francis, who dined there yesterday, the prince was very gay. . . . There were twenty at dinner – no politicks – but still Francis says he thinks, from the language of the equerries and understrappers, that the campaign in Portugal and Lord Wellington begin to be out of fashion with the Regent.

Nov. 1st. – We were at the Pavilion last night – the prince came out of the dining-room. He was in his best humour, bowed and spoke to all of us, and looked uncommonly well, tho' very fat. He was in his full Field Marshal's uniform. He remained quite as cheerful and full of fun to the last – half past twelve – asked after Mrs Creevey's health, and nodded and spoke when he passed us. The Duke of Cumberland was in the regimentals of his own Hussars, looked really hideous, everybody trying to be rude to him – not standing when he came near them. The officers of the prince's regiment had all dined with him, and looked very ornamental monkeys in their red breeches with gold fringe and yellow boots . . .

Nov. 2nd. – We were again at the Pavilion last night. . . . The Regent sat in the Musick Room almost all the time between Viotti, the famous violin player, and Lady Jane Houston, and he went on for hours beating his thighs the proper time for the band, and singing out aloud, and looking about for accompaniment from Viotti and Lady Jane. It was a curious sight to see a Regent thus employed, but he seemed in high good humour. . . . There is nothing like a Minister about him, nor yet any of his old political friends or advisers – no Sheridan, Moira or Hutchinson. Yarmouth and the Duke of Cumberland are always on the spot, and no doubt are his real advisers; but in publick they are mute, and there is no intercourse between the Regent and them. Sir Philip Francis is the only one of his old set here, but he is not here on the Prince's invitation, nor in his suite, and is evidently slighted. Tom Stepney and I last night calculated that Francis and Lord Keith made out 150 years of age between them, and yet they are both here upon their preferment with the Regent – the first, one of the cleverest men one knows, and the other, one of the richest. What a capital libel on mankind! Frances said to me to-day: – 'Well, I am invited to dinner to-day, and that is perhaps all I shall get after two and twenty years' service.' What infernal folly for such a person to have put himself in the way of making so humiliating a confession.

Nov. 5th. – We were at the prince's both last night and the night before (Sunday). . . . The Regent was again all night in the Musick Room, and not content with presiding over the

Band, but actually singing, and very loud too. Last night we were reduced to a smaller party than ever, and Mrs Creevey was well enough to go with me and her daughters for the first time. Nothing could be kinder than the prince's manner to her. When he first saw her coming into the drawing-room, he went up and took hold of both her hands, shook them heartily, made her sit down directly, asked her all about her health, and expressed his pleasure at seeing her look so much better than he expected. Upon her saying she was glad to see him looking so well, he said gravely he was getting old and blind. When she she said she was glad on account of his health that he kept his rooms cooler than he used to do, he said he was quite altered in that respect – that he used to be always *chilly*, and was now never so – that he never had a fire even in his bedroom, and slept with one blanket and sheet only. . . .

Nov. 9th. – Yesterday was the last day of the prince's stay at this place, and, contrary to my expectation, I was invited to dinner. I sat opposite to him, next to Ossulston, and we were the only persons there at all marked by opposition to his appointment of his brother the Duke of York, or to the Government generally, since he has been Regent. He began an old joke at dinner with me about poor Fonblanque, with whom I had dined six years ago at the pavilion . . . [when] the prince and we all got drunk, and he was always used to say it was the merriest day he ever spent. However, it was soon dropped yesterday.

The Duke of Cumberland and Yarmouth never spoke.

LIFE AT CARLTON HOUSE

From The Reminiscences of Captain Gronow*:*

Colonel Palmer, as a result of helping a damosel in distress, becomes the proud owner of an estate in the Bordeaux region:
Palmer, conscious of his inaptitude for business, looked around him for an active agent, and believed he had found one in a Mr Gray, a man of captivating manners and good connections, but almost as useless a person as the general himself.

Fully confident in his own abilities, Gray had already been concerned in many speculations, but not one of them had ever succeeded and all had led to the demolition of large fortunes. Plausible in his address and possessing many of those superficial qualities that please the multitude, he appeared to be able to secure for the claret – which was the production of the estate – a large *clientèle*. Palmer's claret, under his auspices, began to be talked of in the clubs and the *bon vivant* was anxious to secure a quantity of this highly-prized wine.

The patronage of the Prince Regent being considered essential, was solicited, and the prince, with his egotistical good nature and from a kindly feeling for Palmer, gave a dinner at Carlton House, when a fair trial was to be given to his claret. A select circle of *gastronomes* was to be present, amongst whom was Lord Yarmouth, well known in those days by the appellation of 'Red-herrings', from his rubicund whiskers, hair, and face, and from the town of Yarmouth deriving its principal support from the importation from Holland of that fish. . . . The wine was produced and found excellent and the spirits of the party ran high, the light wine animating them without intoxication. The prince was delighted, and, as usual upon such occasions, told some of his best stories, quoted Shakespeare, and was particularly happy upon the bouquet of the wine as suited 'to the holy Palmer's kiss'.

Lord Yarmouth alone sat in moody silence, and, on being questioned as to the cause, replied that whenever he dined at his Royal Highness's table, he drank a claret which he much preferred – that which was furnished by Carbonell. The prince immediately ordered a bottle of this wine, and to give them an opportunity of testing the difference, he desired that some anchovy sandwiches should be served up. Carbonell's wine was placed upon the table: it was a claret made expressly for the London market well-dashed with Hermitage and infinitely more to the taste of the Englishmen than the delicately-flavoured wine they had been drinking. The banquet terminated in the prince declaring his own wine superior to that of Palmer's and suggesting that he should try some experiments on his estate to obtain a better wine. Palmer came from Carlton House much mortified . . .

A curious accident brought Brummell again to the dinner table of his royal patron; he was asked one night at White's to take a hand at whist, when he won from George Harley Drummond £20,000. This circumstance having been related by the Duke of York to the Prince of Wales, the Beau was again invited to Carlton House. At the commencement of the dinner, matters went off smoothly, but Brummell, in his joy at finding himself with his old friend, became excited and drank too much wine. His Royal Highness – who wanted to pay off Brummell for an insult he had received at Lady Cholmondeley's ball, when the Beau, turning towards the Prince, said to Lady Worcester, 'Who is your fat friend?' – had invited him to dinner merely out of a desire for revenge. The Prince therefore pretended to be affronted with Brummell's hilarity, and said to his brother, the Duke of York, who was present, 'I think we had better order Mr Brummell's carriage before he gets drunk'. Whereupon he rang the bell, and Brummell left the royal presence . . .

In 1813 an open-air fête was held in honour of the battle of Vittoria:
This was the first day that her Royal Highness the Princess Charlotte appeared in public. She was a young lady of more than ordinary personal attractions; her features were regular and her complexion fair, with the rich bloom of youthful beauty; her eyes were blue and very expressive and her hair was abundant and of that peculiar light brown which merges into the golden: in fact, such hair as the Middle-Age Italian painters associate with their conceptions of the Madonna. In figure her Royal Highness was somewhat over the ordinary height of women, but finely proportioned and well developed. Her manners were remarkable for a simplicity and good-nature which would have won admiration and invited affection in the most humble walks of life. She created universal admiration, and I may say a feeling of national pride, amongst all who attended the ball.

The Prince Regent entered the gardens giving his arm to the queen, the rest of the royal family following. Tents had been erected in various parts of the grounds, where the bands of the

Guards were stationed. The weather was magnificent, a circumstance which contributed to show off the admirable arrangements of Sir Benjamin Bloomfield, to whom had been deputed the organization of the *fête*, which commenced by dancing on the lawn.

The Princess Charlotte honoured with her presence two dances. In the first she accepted the hand of the late Duke of Devonshire, and in the second that of the Earl of Aboyne, who had danced with Marie Antoinette, and who, as Lord Huntly, lived long enough to dance with Queen Victoria. The princess entered so much into the spirit of the *fête* as to ask for the then fashionable Scotch dances. The prince was dressed in the Windsor uniform and wore the garter and star. He made himself very amiable, and conversed much . . . Altogether, the *fête* was a memorable event.

IN AN IDLE MOMENT

From The Memoirs of Harriet Wilson:

I wonder, thought I, what sort of a nightcap the Prince of Wales wears? Then I went on to wonder whether the Prince of Wales would think me so beautiful as Frederick Lamb did? Next I reflected that Frederick Lamb was younger than the Prince; but then, again, a Prince of Wales!!!

I was undecided: my heart began to soften. I thought of my dear mother, and wished I had never left her. It was too late, however, now. My father would not suffer me to return; and as to passing my life, or any more of it, with Craven, cotton nightcap and all, it was death! He never once made me laugh, nor said nor did anything to please me.

Thus musing, I listlessly turned over my writing-book, half in the humour to address the Prince of Wales. A sheet of paper, covered with Lord Craven's cocoa trees, decided me; and I wrote the following letter, which I addressed to the prince.

BRIGHTON

I am told that I am very beautiful, so, perhaps, you would like to see me; and I wish that, since so many are disposed to love me, one, for in the humility of my heart I should be quite satisfied with one, would be at the pains to make me love him. In the mean time, this is all very dull work, Sir, and worse even than being at home with my father: so, if you pity me, and believe you could make me in love with you, write to me, and direct to the post-office here.

By return of post, I received an answer nearly to this effect: I believe, from Colonel Thomas.

Miss Wilson's letter has been received by the noble individual to whom it was addressed. If Miss Wilson will come to town, she may have an interview, by directing her letter as before.

I answered this note directly, addressing my letter to the Prince of Wales.

SIR,
To travel fifty-two miles, this bad weather, merely to see a man, with only the given number of legs, arms, fingers, etc., would, you must admit, be madness, in a girl like myself, surrounded by humble admirers, who are ever ready to travel any distance for the honour of kissing the tip of her little finger; but if you can prove to me that you are one bit better than any man who may be ready to attend my bidding, I'll e'en start for London directly. So, if you can do anything better, in the way of pleasing a lady, than ordinary men, write directly: if not, adieu, Monsieur le Prince.

I won't say Yours,
By day or night, or any kind of light;
Because you are too impudent.

THE ROYAL MARRIAGE

Gronow's dislike of the woman chosen for 'Prinny' was unequivocal:
The Princess of Wales was one of the most unattractive and almost repulsive women for an elegant minded man that could well have been found amongst German royalty . . .

Joseph Nightingale, in the Memoirs of the Public and Private Life of Queen Caroline, *championed the queen's cause, but in his account of the coronation she inevitably lacked dignity:*
The ceremony of the coronation of George IV says a respectable evening paper of the time, commenced with the military occupations of London. About midnight, the troops which had been collected in the metropolis and its neighbourhood, were

put in motion; and, before one o'clock in the morning, a body of infantry, three or four thousand strong, had assembled in St James's Park. This body was immediately filed off, in detachments, to secure the entrances into the town, and to take up commanding positions in the principal streets. Strong guards were placed at Hyde Park corner, Storey's Gate, the foot of Westminster bridge, etc.; while pickets of still greater force were sent out in several directions, particularly to Portman-street barracks, Knightsbridge barracks, and the King's Mews. Fifteen hundred men occupied the platform in Palace-yard, and two companies of grenadiers were posted in Westminster Abbey. In addition to these guards and detachments, which were all composed of infantry, two thousand cavalry were stationed in several quarters of the town, and kept up a regular chain of communication between the different posts. The cuirasses of the Oxford Blues gleamed in one direction, those of the Life Guards in another. In addition to the guards and detachments of the regular troops, the Light Horse Volunteers, the Surrey, the Berks and Bucks Yeomanry, with the Honourable Artillery Company, were on duty, occupying the passes into the metropolis, or patrolling the principal streets. All these military arrangements were completed before two o'clock in the morning. The dawn of day saw the metropolis of England in military occupation; and had a stranger, not possessed of any previous knowledge of the events which had been passing, approached at that moment, he might have mistaken London for a conquered city, in which the governing powers were at war with the people.

In spite of all these precautions, the queen proceeded in state to Westminster Abbey:

Her Majesty, when she alighted, was accompanied by Lady Hood and Lady Hamilton, and leaned upon the arm of Lord Hood. On reaching the door, however, the mistake was discovered, and the group returned. Her Majesty was now surrounded by a great number of persons, who followed her along the side of the platform till she reached the steps by which persons having Peers' tickets were permitted to ascend. There she instantly mounted, followed by her suite, and leaning on Lord Hood. On reaching the platform, the soldiery were drawn across the passage, and an officer advanced and asked for the tickets. Lord Hood said, he had authority to be there, and at the same time took a paper from his pocket. On presenting it, without examination her Majesty was permitted to pass. She then crossed the platform, and descended on the other side. As she proceeded, several constables went before her, and the populace surrounded her on all sides. The constables and people having led the way towards the passage leading to the kitchen, her Majesty followed; but the gate being shut, and an explanation given of the place at which she had arrived, Lord Hood said her Majesty's desire was not to go into the Hall, but to go to Poet's Corner, with the view of gaining admission to the Abbey. Thither she was instantly conducted, through an opening in the covered way. On arriving at the place where tickets were received, Lord Hood demanded admission for the Queen.

The door-keeper said, that his instructions were to admit no person without a Peer's ticket.

Lord Hood – 'Did you ever hear of a Queen being asked for a ticket before? This is your Queen.'

The door-keeper said that his orders were general, and without any exceptions. He had never been in a similar situation before, and could say nothing as to the propriety or impropriety of refusing her Majesty admission.

Lord Hood. – 'I present to you your Queen, do you refuse her admission?'

Her Majesty added, that she was his Queen, and desired to be permitted to pass.

The door-keeper repeated that his orders were peremptory – and said, however reluctant he might be, he could not suffer her Majesty to pass without a ticket.

Lord Hood. – 'I have a ticket.'

Door-keeper. – 'Upon producing it I will permit you to pass.'

Lord Hood then took from his pocket one ticket for the Abbey, for a Mr Wellington, which he tendered to the door-keeper.

The door-keeper said that it would admit but one individual.

Lord Hood then asked her Majesty if she would enter alone?

Her Majesty hesitated – upon which

Lord Hood asked, whether there had not been some preparations made for her Majesty's reception.

The door-keeper answered in the negative.

Lord Hood. – 'Then I am to understand you refuse your Queen admittance to Westminster Abbey?'

The door-keeper said he was ready to admit her Majesty with a ticket, but not without.

After a short consultation with her Majesty, as to whether she would go into the Abbey alone, or not – her Majesty declined – and it was resolved, having been refused admission to the Cathedral church of Westminster, that she should return to her carriage.

As she turned round to quit the spot, some persons in the door-way burst into a vulgar laugh of derision. Her Majesty looked at them contemptuously; and Lord Hood observed, that in such a place he expected to have met with decorous conduct at least towards a Sovereign – instead of that she had been denied her indubitable right, and been treated, not only in an ill-mannered, but in an unmanly way.

Her Majesty then turned about, and passed through a group of fashionable women, who were going to the Abbey with tickets, but who did not take the slightest notice of her. Her Majesty was followed by a crowd to the platform, some of whom were approving and some disapproving her conduct. On entering her carriage, there was considerable disapprobation, intermingled with cries of 'shame, shame,' 'off, off;' but other parts of the populace repeated the cries of 'the Queen, the Queen,' with great enthusiasm. Her Majesty was elegantly dressed in a muslim slip, on a petticoat of silver brocade. She wore a small purple scarf, and had a splendid diamond bandeau on her head, with feathers.

Gronow saw the coronation from a different angle:

At this gorgeous solemnity it fell to my lot to be on guard on the platform along which the royal procession had to pass in order to reach the Abbey. The crowd that had congregated in this locality exceeded anything I had ever before seen: struggling, fighting, shrieking, and laughing were the order of the day among this motley assemblage. Little Townsend, the chief police officer of Bow Street, with his flaxen wig and broad-brimmed hat, was to be seen hurrying from one end of the platform to the other, assuming immense importance. On the approach of the *cortège* you heard the officious person, 'dressed with a little brief authority', hallooing with all his might, 'Gentlemen and ladies, take care of your pockets, for you are surrounded by thieves', and hearty laughter responded to Mr Townsend's salutary advice.

When the procession was seen to approach and the royal canopy came in sight, those below the platform were straining with all their might to get a peep at the Sovereign and the confusion at this moment can be better imagined than described. The pickpockets, of course, had availed themselves of the confusion and in the twinkling of an eye there were more watches and purses snatched from the pockets of his majesty's loyal subjects than perhaps on any previous occasion.

Amidst the crowd a respectable gentleman from the Principality hallooed out in his provincial tongue, 'Mr Townsend, Mr Townsend, I have been robbed of my gold watch and purse, containing all my money. What am I to do? What am I to do to get home? I have come two hundred miles to see this sight, and instead of receiving satisfaction or hospitality I am robbed by those cut-throats called "the swell mob".' This eloquent speech had a very different effect upon the mob than the poor Welshman had reason the expect, for all of a sudden the refrain of the song of [*Home*,] *Sweet Home* was shouted by a thousand voices; and the mob bawled out, 'Go back to your goats, my good fellow'. The indignities that were heaped upon this unfortunate gentleman during the royal procession, and his appearance after the king had passed, created pity in the minds of all honest persons who witnessed this disgusting scene: his hat was beaten over his eyes, and his coat, neckcloth, etc, were torn off his body. For there were no police in those days, and with the exception of a few constables and some soldiers there was no force to prevent the metropolis from being burnt to the ground, if it had pleased the mob to have set it on fire.

Creevey leaves us with this last impression:
Edinburgh 17 August 1822
... I send you a *Scotsman* [newspaper], the Account in which as to the king is pretty correct. He has been received by the people in the most respectful and orderly manner. All have turn'd out in their holiday cloaths, and in numbers which are hardly credible. ... I have been much disappointed to-day with the levee. ... There was nothing interesting or imposing about it. A vast crowd, with barely standing room for two hours: afterwards moved to the Presence Chamber, where no one was for a minute. ... The king did not seem to move a muscle, and we all asked each other, when we came away, what had made us take so much trouble. He was dressed in tartan. Sir Walter Scott has ridiculously made us appear to be a nation of Highlanders, and the bagpipe and the tartan are the order of the day.

QUEEN VICTORIA

(b. 1819, reigned 1837–1901)

The most shattering blow of Queen Victoria's life occurred on 14 December 1861 when her beloved husband, Prince Albert of Saxe-Coburg, died from typhoid fever. For many years after her pleasures were purely nostalgic and she particularly enjoyed reading the journal she had kept during many glorious Highland holidays with Albert at her side. Eventually she was persuaded to publish Leaves from the Journal of Our Life in the Highlands, *and this extract is a typical example of her simple, straightforward style and her almost naive delight in 'homely' pleasures:*

FÊTE TO MEMBERS OF THE BRITISH ASSOCIATION

22 September 1859: The morning dawned brightly. Suddenly a very high wind arose which alarmed us, but yet it looked bright, and we hoped the wind would keep off the rain; but after breakfast, while watching the preparations, showers began, and from half-past eleven a fearful down-pour, with that white curtain-like appearance which is so alarming; and this lasted till half-past twelve. I was in despair; but at length it began to clear, just as the neighbours with their families, and some of the farmers opposite (the Herrons, Duncans, Brown's father and brothers) arrived, and then came the huge omnibuses and carriages laden with 'philosophers.' At two o'clock we were all ready. Albert and the boys were in their kilts, and I and the girls in royal Stuart skirts and shawls over black velvet bodices.

It was a beautiful sight in spite of the frequent slight showers which at first tormented us, and the very high cold wind. There were gleams of sunshine, which, with the Highlanders in their brilliant and picturesque dresses, the wild notes of the pipes, the band, and the beautiful background of mountains, rendered the scene wild and striking in the extreme. The Farquharson's men headed by Colonel Farquharson, the Duff's by Lord Fife, and the Forbes's men by Sir Charles Forbes, had all marched on the ground before we came out, and were drawn up just opposite to us, and the spectators (the people of the country) behind them. We stood on the terrace, the company near us, and the 'savants,' also, on either side of us, and along the slopes, on the grounds. The games began about three o'clock:

1. 'Throwing the Hammer.'
2. 'Tossing the Caber.'
3. 'Putting the Stone.'

We gave prizes to the three best in each of the games. We walked along the terrace to the large marquee, talking to the people, to where the men were 'putting the stone.' After this returned to the upper terrace, to see the race, a pretty wild sight; but the men looked very cold, with nothing but their shirts and kilts on; they ran beautifully. They wrapped plaids round themselves, and then came to receive the prizes from me. Last of all came the dancing – reels and 'Ghillie Callum'. The latter the judges could not make up their minds about; it was danced over and over again; and at last they left out the best dancer of all! They said he danced 'too well!' The dancing over, we left amid the loud cheers of the people. It was then about half-past five.